Every sensitive soul is concerned for their family—especially in these days so packed with challenges ready to crush the best and brightest hopes for their well-being. I commend Arni Jacobson for providing this book—a gift for caring parents and relatives to take practical steps that can make the ultimate difference to access the love, grace, and power of God on their behalf.

—Jack W. Hayford
Founding Pastor, The Church On The Way
Chancellor, The King's College and Seminary

If there is such a thing as an expert in soul-winning, Arni Jacobson would clearly be on the list—in fact, near the top. His simple book *Five Keys to Reaching Your Family for Christ* is one of the most needed books for Christian families in our troubled culture of today. You need this book—even if it is to help rescue and restore other broken families that will cross your path.

—Dick Eastman
International President
Every Home for Christ

Never before have we needed this book more than right now. It is a biblical plan to reach our families for Christ. Arni Jacobson's insight will bring new hope for your efforts to lead your family to Jesus.

—Steve Munsey
Senior Pastor, Family Worship Center
Munster, Indiana

Arni Jacobson has hit the nail on the head with his latest book. As I read *Five Keys to Leading Your Family to Christ* I found myself shaking my head "yes" to each of the five keys. This is a must-read for everyone praying for a family member to come to the Lord.

—Pastor Rich Wilkerson
Evangelist, Author, and Pastor
Trinity Church, Miami, Florida

Arni Jacobson's *Five Keys to Leading Your Family to Christ* is a readable and digestible book that will be the faith-builder you need. It comes out of the laboratory of practice and success.

—Glen D. Cole
Pastor, Trinity Life Center
Sacramento, California

This book is a must-read for anyone interested in seeing their loved ones come to saving faith in Christ. The practices covered in this book are biblical, down-to-earth, and come from a lifelong soul-winner who knows what evangelism is all about.

—Pastor Chris Pena
Foundation Christian Ministries

My dear friend, Arni, has hit another home run! *Five Keys to Reaching Your Family for Christ* contains simple, yet profound wisdom that every believer has been looking for to help them lead their loved ones along the path to salvation. If you have struggled with the "how to" or "why it hasn't happened yet," this book will provide the answers and direction you need!

—DICK BERNAL
PASTOR, JUBILEE CHRISTIAN CENTER, SAN JOSE, CA

Arni Jacobson is an extremely successful pastor and church planter. He has established and pastored churches with thousands of members and is currently ministering to pastors and leaders across our nation and around the world. He is a friend, a ministry partner, and an inspiration to others. His qualifications in writing a book on reaching others for Christ are evident in the people whom he has personally led to Christ. From bankers, lawyers, and professional sports figures to families and friends, Arni has a gift for sharing his personal experience in a way that makes others want to have the same experience. Recognizing the uniqueness of family culture, Arni shares five practical keys that provide an effective, spiritual approach to reach our families for Christ.

These five keys are for anyone who wants to see their family members experience life in Christ. For this reason, it is a great privilege to recommend this book.

—STEVE RIGGLE
SENIOR PASTOR, GRACE COMMUNITY CHURCH,
HOUSTON, TX
PRESIDENT, GRACE INTERNATIONAL

5 KEYS

TO REACHING
YOUR FAMILY
FOR CHRIST

ARNI JACOBSON

CREATION HOUSE
A STRANG COMPANY

Five Keys to Reaching Your Family for Christ
by Arni Jacobson
Published by Creation House
A Strang Company
600 Rinehart Road
Lake Mary, Florida 32746
www.strangbookgroup.com

Design Director: Bill Johnson

Cover design by Amanda Potter

Library of Congress Control Number: 2009935576
International Standard Book Number:
978-1-59979-940-7

First Edition

09 10 11 12 13 — 987654321
Printed in the United States of America

DEDICATION

I dedicate this book to my family—my wife, Jan; my son, Chad; his wife, Amanda; their two sons, Ethan and Collin; my daughter, Brooke; and her husband; Josh. I also dedicate this book to my sister, Judy, to whom I owe my place in heaven and my passion for salvation.

Acknowledgments

THIS BOOK COULD NOT have been birthed without the dedicated help and expertise of my friend, Robert Mims. He took my handwritten notes, many hours of personal meetings, and recorded teachings to construct this book. Robert Mims can be contacted at mimsmedia.com if you are looking for a godly man to help construct your manuscript.

My daughter, Brooke, and my son-in-law, Josh, for helping keep me on task and working with me on deadlines.

To my new friend, Kim Edlin, for her brilliant help and strategy in marketing.

Cathy Tonn, a close family friend, who has greatly helped expedite the release of this book in so many ways.

The team at Creation House and Strang Publishers for being fantastic partners to work with.

To the pastors and ministry leaders who understood the importance of this message and felt prompted to endorse this book.

I also want to thank all of those special people who allowed us inside their families and shared their exciting and sometimes painful stories to encourage us in seeing the fulfillment of the Acts 16:31 promise.

To Reverend Nat Olson, who introduced me to Acts 16:31 in the early 1970s and gave me confidence that my family could be saved.

To Pastor John Wilkerson, who led my sister to Christ, and was my spiritual backing in my early years as a Christian.

To Jesus Christ, who died for my sins and gave Himself for my family and yours.

CONTENTS

Introduction 1

1 Key No. 1: Pray Every Day for Your
Unsaved Family Members 10

2 Key No. 2: Stand Strong Against Satan
(Expect Demonic Opposition) 21

3 Key No. 3: Expect an Uproar in Your
Family 33

4 Key No. 4: Create an Environment of
Worship to Build Your Boldness 43

5 Key No. 5: Believe from the Depths of Your
Heart Your Family Will Come to Christ 51

6 Your Five Keys Spiritual Tool Chest 58

"Five Keys to Reaching Your Family for Christ"
Strategy Card 64

More Encouragement for the Journey 65

INTRODUCTION

WORRY ETCHED THEIR FACES. Their eyes red with tears, John and Elaine sighed, slumped behind cups of bitter coffee, and faced each other across the kitchen table. The cause of distress: their daughter, Janna, once their pride and joy. She was a good Christian girl, everyone would say; active in the youth group, a good student, caring, and known for her open, innocent smile.

Then she went off to college. The calls and letters home became less frequent, and when she did communicate, the tone was uncharacteristically distant and, somehow, hard. Janna no longer went to church, saying she "needed a break from all that." Stories began to trickle back from friends of missed classes, drinking, and a wild party life. When confronted, she not only failed to deny the reports but also seemed proud of her 180-degree change in behavior. And now this letter Elaine held in her hand—*expulsion*.

"Honey, you need to come back to the Lord," Elaine had just pleaded with her daughter on the phone. Janna had huffed in anger and then hung up. Elaine felt hopeless and alone, even as her husband reached for her hand. "What do we do, Lord?" she cried.

Paul and Linda had raised their son, Liam, in a good Bible-believing church, and when he married Heather, she seemed nice enough. But Heather, while respectful of their "born again" convictions, did not share them. And now it appeared their grandson, Josh, had no interest in Christ either.

When Liam found marijuana and a wad of unexplained cash hidden in Josh's closet, he had erupted in anger—and Josh had run out of the house. That had been a week ago, and there had been no word since. Then came the call from Liam: Josh was in jail.

The aging couple had prayed for their son's marriage and their increasingly rebellious grandson for months, but things just seemed to get worse. "What else can we do, honey?" Paul asked Linda. She shook her head, answering, "I don't know, Paul, but there has to be something. What does God want for us to do? We can't lose our grandson!"

It had been five years since the divorce, but the scars were still fresh for Pete and his sister, Marilyn, now both grown and on their own. Their mom and dad still bitterly competed for their attention, and visits to either of them always became a point of contention for the other. If not for their shared acceptance of Christ, the siblings would truly feel lost.

Both Pete and Marilyn had tried to share their faith with their folks. Mom would say, "That's nice for you, but I don't need it." Dad was more abrupt: "Whatever. If you need a crutch, fine; I don't. Besides, where was God when your mother left me?"

Marilyn sobbed as Pete listened on the phone. "Mom and Dad aren't getting any younger. What if they die without knowing Christ? We would never see them again!" she cried.

"We've got to have faith, sis. But I know it's hard. It seems our prayers are going unanswered. I just don't know what else to do!" he said.

Do you find yourself nodding, familiar with one or more of the situations in the scenarios above? Do you have loved ones who have strayed from or have yet to make a decision for Christ?

If the answer is yes, then this book, *Five Keys to Reaching Your Family for Christ*, is for you.

My spirit has been pregnant with this book for more than thirty years—rather a long gestation period, I suppose—but I believe that its long-awaited birth will profoundly affect the body of Christ. It is my prayer and deepest desire that *Five Keys to Reaching Your Family for Christ* will encourage and give strength and renewed hope to believers who yearn to see their sons and daughters, mothers and fathers, brothers and sisters, and others come to Jesus.

That's what this little book is all about. It is meant to be an easy-to-read yet powerful and straight-forward tool through which the Holy Spirit will bring many to a personal knowledge of Christ.

I was born again on January 3, 1967, led to the Lord in a restaurant while having coffee with the Rev. John Wilkerson, my sister's pastor. My sister, Judy Doxtater, had made her own commitment to Christ in 1964 while battling cancer (Hodgkin's disease).

That was a battle she would eventually lose, but she made spiritual inroads during that fight that had eternal impact. Judy's salvation, testimony, and her eventual death were catalysts to a chain reaction of people coming to Jesus in our family—including me, though belatedly.

From that starting point through what has now been some four decades of ministry, I will share with you what I have learned from Scripture and experience about the keys to reaching your family—and friends and coworkers, too—for the Savior.

Nothing is more painful to a child of God than knowing one's unsaved relatives are facing the possibility of an eternity in hell, separated forever from the light, love, and presence of our Creator. Seeing them saved should be a desire beating strong in the heart of any serious believer.

In 1971, on my first assignment out of Bible college, I met a man named Nat Olson, who would play an important role in putting me on the Five Keys path and developing this message that I share with you now.

Nat and his family attended Bethel Tabernacle Church in Milwaukee, Wisconsin. This strongly ethnic German congregation invited my wife, Jan, and me to serve as youth and education pastors. That's where we met Nat, and our friendship turned out to be a defining, God-ordained intersection in a spiritual journey Jan and I were just beginning.

Actually, Nat, who passed away in 2001 at age sixty-five, made a lasting impact on everyone he met. He was the poster child for a "people person" and a passionate Christian. He made sharing the love of Jesus Christ a way of life. Indeed, Nat, who was raised in a pastor's home, began telling people about Jesus when he was just five years old!

His father, Pete (known as "the singing evange-list"), hosted a daily radio broadcast that aired for nearly forty years in Canada and the U.S. Nat was featured in this program and soon began hosting his own children's show. Encouraged by his moth-er's love of poetry, Nat began to develop his gift of writing. By age fifteen he was a published author, and he would go on to write more than a dozen other books in all.

A 1958 graduate of Central Bible Institute (now Central Bible College), he married Shirley Bagley later that year. Along with ministering in churches throughout the country, Nat served as scriptwriter for the *Haven of Rest* radio broadcast in Hollywood, California, for nine years.

In 1970, he moved his family to Wisconsin, where he founded Familytime Ministries. He hosted a daily radio broadcast of the same name and also provided counseling services to local listeners.

It was through Familytime that I was introduced to Nat's core scripture verse, Acts 16:31: "Believe in the Lord Jesus, and you will be saved—you and your household."

Since the day I accepted Christ, I have been a soul-winner, zealous to reach the lost. Nat was of the same cut, his heart particularly tender toward reaching lost family members. So, over the years I have made it a practice to encourage people to read and claim that biblical promise in Acts 16:31. I have seen many of my own family come to Christ, and I stand on that verse.

Recently, God really spoke to my heart from the entire passage that contains that key promise, Acts 16:16–34. This occurred in Memphis, Tennessee, where I was preaching on God's provision to and blessing of the prophet Nehemiah, my topic in a previous book, *The Favor Factor*.*

My good friend Pastor Ron Woods sprang something of a surprise on me. "So, Arni, what are you going to be speaking on Sunday night?" he asked. I had come prepared to speak Sunday morning, but this second engagement took me unawares. Still, I blurted out an answer: "Family evangelism."

At least I had a nice, general topic everyone could relate to, right? What I didn't have, though, was a sermon. Back in my motel room that Sunday afternoon, I prayed for guidance and inspiration—and God gave me the Five Keys. That sermon was the birth of the message—preached to thousands in churches around the world since—and now this book.

Everywhere I've spoken on the Five Keys, one of the first things people have asked is, "Where's the

---

* Arni Jacobson, *The Favor Factor* (Lake Mary, FL: Charisma House, 2007).

book to go with the message? We want to know more!" It was a question only amplified when I appeared in April 2009 on the Trinity Broadcasting Network's *Praise the Lord* program, hosted by Pastor Steve Munsey and his son, Kent.

Once again, the discussion was on the Favor Factor. But the ground quickly changed—a Holy Spirit thing, I believe—as I mentioned that God's favor comes when we lead people to Christ. The conversation quickly took a detour, moving into my message on the Five Keys and plans for this book.

Within minutes of my Web site (www. arnijacobson.com) being flashed for just a few seconds on the TBN screen, hundreds of visitors logged on to ask how to get the book. Remember how earlier in this introduction I used pregnancy as a metaphor for the Five Keys message? Well, that was the moment the water broke! Suddenly, God had put the birth of this book on the fast track.

As you read and apply the Five Keys principles to your own family, let's believe God together for a great harvest of souls and families united in Christ!

Remember, "God is not a man, that he should lie, nor a son of man, that he should change his mind," as Numbers 23:19 tells us. So, we can believe the Acts 16:31 promise, "Believe in the Lord Jesus, and you will be saved—you and your household."

In the following chapters you will learn these God-given, God-promised principles for seeing your family come to Christ. (Remember, it's a promise from God!)

1. *Pray* every day for your unsaved family members.

2. *Stand* strong against Satan.

3. *Expect* an exciting uproar in your family.

4. *Create* an environment of worship to build your boldness.

5. *Believe* from the depths of your heart that your family will come to Christ.

CHAPTER 1

KEY NO. 1

PRAY EVERY DAY FOR YOUR UNSAVED FAMILY MEMBERS

ACTS 16:16 SAYS, "Now it happened, as we went to prayer…" (NKJV). The apostle Paul, joined by a Jerusalem disciple, Silas; Luke, the physician and writer; and the young Timothy, were heading to the Gangites River outside the Roman province town of Philippi to pray with the area's small number of other Jews. They didn't know they were stepping into spiritual and physical trials that would put them face-to-face with the grim reaper.

More on that later. For now, let's consider that word *happened*. I love that word. You might say I'm a "happening" kind of guy. I love it when things happen in God! So, here's that favorite word, right at the beginning of this amazing passage of Scripture that ushers us onto the path of the Five Keys— *happened*. It also stirs fond memories of that classic

Bill Gaither song "He Touched Me" and its refrain, which describes how one touch from God leaves us whole.

Leading your family to Christ starts with prayer. That's how it begins to *happen*. It is prayer that will open the door to release God's promises. It is as simple—and profound—as that; it is a truth that God has been driving into my heart.

I challenge you: make a list of your unsaved family members. (You may find a template for this kind of prayer list at the end of this book.) Pray daily for their salvation. Do it first thing in the morning. Enlist a prayer partner, too, remembering another godly promise: "For where two or three come together in my name, there am I with them" (Matt. 18:20). I also like how *The Message* Bible puts it: "When two of you get together on anything at all on earth and make a prayer of it, my Father in heaven goes into action. And when...you are together because of me, you can be sure that I'll be there."

A good example of just this assurance from the Lord came when a close friend of mine, the Rev. Gary Batt, was awakened by the spirit of the Lord. He had been praying with me all along about the Five Keys message, and suddenly the Lord brought to his mind these words: "Tell Arni that many of my children have given up and are not praying for their relatives! Tell them to start praying again, and breakthroughs will come!"

There are many ways you can do this, too. For example, when I shared the Five Keys message at the Church on the Green in Sun City, Arizona, I met several sweet retired ladies there who had begun an Internet-based ministry called Moms United for Prayer at www.mom-interceding.blogspot.com. In their blog's introduction, the leader of these ladies, Carolyn Schwenk, describes herself as a minister's daughter, happily married mother, grandmother, great-grandmother, and retired nurse now living with her husband in a retirement community. But, she goes on to explain, she has *not* retired from serving God—or lifting her family and others' loved ones up in prayer.

"A couple of years ago, the Holy Spirit birthed into my heart a passion to pray and to intercede for the salvation of our church family's children who have left the faith. I am blessed with a small group of beautiful praying sisters," Carolyn writes. "Together we have been praying one morning per week…for our children and grandkids that are unsaved. We stand in prayer against spiritual darkness, believing God to bless each one of them with a desire and passion to serve Him."

Her blog also contains links to Christian music, videos, and numerous other faith-building Web sites. But Carolyn's passion—and that of other ladies who have joined her on their knees—is praying for believers' unsaved family members.

These spiritual warriors show that praying moms and grandmoms have and always will be able to "shake the kingdom," as the saying goes. My own mother found Christ in her fifties; she was led to the Lord, along with my father, by my sister, Judy, from her hospital room shortly before Judy's death at age 26.

For our family, the Acts 16:34 chain reaction began at that point.

Now, we Jacobsons had certainly *heard* about Jesus before. We were, after all, raised in a mainstream Protestant denomination. But that church had become so mired in its centuries of ritual and tradition that it no longer really preached a personal, born-again, John 3:16 kind of salvation experience.

Today, looking back at the family members who came to know Christ personally because of the spiritual tsunami my sister's prayers and witnessing triggered, I wonder whose prayer list my parents, Judy, my brothers, and myself were on.

Long ago as I pondered that question, my memory banks were peeled back to a conversation I had with my father. He told me about my great-grandmother Wilhelmina Jacobson, an active member of a Baptist church. Great-grandma had come to this country from Sweden in the 1800s, settling in Door County, Wisconsin. (If you've ever been to Door County, it looks a lot like Sweden, especially in the winter, with one of the Great Lakes wrapping around a Nordic peninsula. It's miserably cold, and there is a lot of snow. Maybe that's why she and the other Swedish immigrants went there—no one else wanted to!)

Great-grandma married and raised her children, including my grandfather, Enoch, to serve the Lord. But when Enoch Jacobson met and married my grandmother, Emma, he joined her church, the same denomination I was to be raised in. Grandpa had turned a page in his spiritual life, and it was away from the clear heaven-or-hell salvation message of his Baptist youth toward a more liberal theology that no longer preached a strong personal commitment to Christ.

When my father, Arnold Jacobson, was a child, he often visited my great-grandma on the farm. She always made sure he heard a simple, clear gospel message: "Arnold, you need to be born again." My dad also remembered hearing this woman of God praying for him when she didn't know he was listening: "Lord, let Arnold come to know Christ, and his children's children, too."

That prayer all those years ago from a little old Swedish woman on her knees in a Door County farmhouse was answered decades later in a Kenosha,

Wisconsin, hospital room. It is also because of an answer to that prayer that I'm writing this book today.

My sister Judy was a young mother, pregnant with her third child, when she noticed a lump on her neck. A biopsy resulted in a medical diagnosis that in 1963 was still a death sentence: advanced Hodgkin's disease. Doctors predicted that at best, using the most aggressive treatment regimens then available, Judy had less than two years to live.

As Judy heard that devastating news, so did the woman in the next hospital bed. Her name was Millie Scott. She was a Christian woman who was moved by her compassion and commitment to the Lord to share her testimony of personal salvation with my crushed sister. Millie then invited Judy to her church, the First Assembly of God in Kenosha.

Judy went to that church and heard the author of *The Cross and the Switchblade*, the Rev. David Wilkerson, speak. At the end of his message he gave an invitation to people to surrender their lives to Christ, and Judy did.

My sister lived three more years, almost twice as long as her doctors had given her under what they considered the best possible medical circumstances. In those extra years God gave her, Judy personally brought more than a hundred people to church to hear the gospel.

My parents were the last people Judy led to the Lord while she was alive. Three days after they prayed the sinner's prayer, Judy passed away. The church had standing room only for her funeral, and the procession of cars that went to the cemetery stretched for miles. She touched many, many lives.

It was four months later, in a Howard Johnson's restaurant in Chicago, that Pastor John Wilkerson (David's cousin) led me to the Lord. I turned out to be Judy's final triumph, and the last one she would have expected to follow her to Christ. Indeed, shortly before she died she had told my brother Dave that she could believe God could save anyone—*except* her hard-drinking, cynical brother Arni, who was so negative about her salvation stories. But God knew that on the inside, I was soft as a marshmallow toward my sister's testimony. Prayer works.

For many years I served on the board of the renowned Yoido Full Gospel Church in Seoul, South Korea. Pastor David Yonggi Cho will tell you he built that church of 830,000 members on prayer. Thousands upon thousands of families in that Asian nation were literally prayed into the kingdom of God. (I'll tell you a bit more about Dr. Cho later on in this book.)

Things happen when you pray! Don't get discouraged. Delays in answers to your prayers for those wandering loved ones are *not* denials.

Let me finish this chapter with a true story from my ministry days in Salt Lake City, Utah, during the 1980s.

Ruth began coming to my church after the death of her husband, a longtime Baptist minister in Utah. Her husband's successor in the pulpit, apparently worried about Ruth's continuing influence, made it clear he did not want this sweet lady in the church that was now his. Hurt but also wanting to give the new minister the fresh start he wanted, Ruth left. She began coming to the church I was pastoring.

Ruth had been raised in upstate New York by godly parents who prayed for her and her brother, John, constantly. Ruth's folks, who ran a bakery, were solid, born-again believers and wanted the same gift of grace to rule their children's lives. Ruth stayed the course and ended up marrying a preacher. (My wife Jan will tell you that makes Ruth a saint!) Johnny, however, fell away from Christ after enlisting in the navy during World War II.

Johnny had been a fine young Christian man up until then and had felt called to the ministry. But by the time the war had ended, he had become a hopeless alcoholic. When he took over the family's business, he ran it into the ground. Next, he lost his own family to divorce. In a few more short years Johnny was wandering the streets in a constant drunken stupor. He was a bum, the kind you see on the streets begging for spare change.

Still, his sister, Ruth, along with their mother and father, continued to pray that their wayward son would finally return to Christ. Johnny's parents passed away not seeing those prayers answered. Decades more passed, and Ruth was now a pastor's widow living in Salt Lake City.

One day, Johnny showed up at her doorstep disheveled and reeking of booze and the filth of the streets. Ruth took Johnny in anyway, making up a room for him in her basement. For a few days at a time Johnny would be sober; then when his Social Security check arrived, he would disappear, drinking himself into unconsciousness. Days later, he would return to Ruth's home, many times stained with his own vomit and excrement.

I often helped Ruth clean him up. She would lovingly nurse him back to sobriety, only to have the drinking cycle repeat itself, time after time. This went on for about six months. Then one Saturday afternoon while I was watching a college football game, right in the middle of it I felt a strong need to go over and see Ruth. She had become close to our family, a surrogate grandmother to our son and daughter and a treasured friend to me and my wife, Jan.

When I arrived in Ruth's driveway she ran out to meet me, a surprised, yet relieved look on her face. "Pastor, I can't believe you're here!" she cried. "I just called Jan. She said you were coming. Pastor, Johnny is dying!"

Ruth told me how she had made her way down to her brother's room and found him lying on his bed, barely alive. Together, we rushed down to his bedside. It was as bad as Ruth had described. Emaciated, cold, and gray, it was clear that Johnny's time was finally and rapidly running out. In a weak voice he kept repeating, "Lord, be merciful to me, a sinner."

With a sense of urgency, I knelt down next to him. "Johnny, would you like to give your life to Christ?" I asked.

"Yes, Pastor Arni," he whispered. And we prayed a simple sinner's prayer right there: "Dear Jesus, I'm a sinner. Come into my life and forgive my sins." This tortured man finally had peace, and the prayers of his long-dead parents had been answered. Literally pushing out his last breath, Johnny said, "Amen," and was gone.

Why this story? To illustrate that godly parents from upstate New York, though they had died in the mid 1950s, had their prayers for a lost son answered decades later.

Can you imagine the scene in heaven as his parents embraced their son, another prodigal who had finally made it home? Johnny *was* home. Like the son Jesus told of in Luke 15:32, this brother "was dead and is alive again; he was lost and is found."

Never give up. *Never.* Delays are not denials when it comes to our petitions to a loving Father for the souls of our loved ones.

No, *never* give up; God doesn't.

Points to remember

- ↢ It all begins with prayer—first thing, every day. If you have given up, start praying right now.

- ↢ Recruit a prayer partner or two. Jesus promises to be there for you.

- ↢ Delay in an answer is not a denial.

CHAPTER 2

KEY NO. 2

STAND STRONG AGAINST SATAN
(EXPECT DEMONIC OPPOSITION)

L ET'S GO BACK TO Acts 16 for a moment and pick up where we left off with Paul, Silas, Timothy, and Luke (who wrote Acts). They had gathered with a small group of other Jews to pray along the Gangites River outside the city of Philippi. Earlier, they met and converted a woman named Lydia there, and then baptized her and her entire family.

This time, though, we read:

> We were met by a slave girl who had a spirit by which she predicted the future. She earned a great deal of money for her owners by fortune-telling. This girl followed Paul and the rest of us, shouting, "These men are servants of the Most High God, who are telling you the way to be saved." She kept

this up for many days. Finally Paul became so troubled that he turned around and said to the spirit, "In the name of Jesus Christ I command you to come out of her!" At that moment the spirit left her.

—ACTS 16:16–18

The Message puts that last part this way: "Paul, finally fed up with her, turned and commanded the spirit that possessed her, 'Out! In the name of Jesus Christ, get out of her!' And it was gone, just like that."

Paul and his band had really gotten themselves in trouble. When that spirit of divination was booted out of that girl, she lost her "gift"—and her owners lost their meal ticket. These enraged psychic businessmen seized Paul and Silas, roughed them up, and dragged them into the marketplace for a hurriedly arranged hearing before the local magistrates. Think *kangaroo court.*

"These men are Jews," they said, firing up anti-Semitism and obviously hoping to stir the emotions generated by the Roman Emperor Claudius's recent ouster of Rome's Jewish community and the empire-wide crackdown on Israelites abroad. "[They] are throwing our city into an uproar by advocating customs unlawful for us Romans to accept or practice," their accusers charged (Acts 16:20–21).

The crowd, with the all-too-eager-to-please magistrates chiming in, attacked Paul and Silas then. Actually, they stripped them naked, flogged them bloody, and then threw them into the fetid, dark inner recesses of the local prison. Inside, Paul and Silas had their feet strapped into stocks. They were deep inside the first century's version of maximum security.

Their companions there in the jail? The worst criminals of those times, most of them under the threat of execution—murderers, rapists, child molesters, and others of their ilk. These were really *bad* guys. And this was a *bad* prison. No nice bunk bed, metal toilet, and sink. No toilets at all, folks, unless you count the trough that ran down along the ground. No showers. No air-filtration system either. Imagine the smell, the rats, bugs, centipedes running through that stuff.

As an uncle of mine used to say, it could gag a maggot on a gut wagon.

So, Paul and Silas were accused of triggering an uproar. Well, an uproar had for sure been set off in Philippi, but it was from angry and vengeful slaveholders who could no longer abuse a demon-possessed girl, and of the outright lies they told against the two men of God. In other words, it was Satan himself who created this uproar, though God was about to turn it around; stay tuned.

As you take your lost loved ones to God in prayer and act on the Five Keys, you, too, can expect an uproar to develop in the form of demonic opposition (and even an uproar in your own family—but more on that to come).

Let me ask you a question: What is the one thing the devil does not want to have happen in your life or in the lives of those you love? That's right, from the very core of Satan's black heart, he cannot stand the idea of God's children being reconciled to their Creator.

It has been that way from the beginning.

> Now the serpent was more crafty than any of the wild animals the LORD God had made. He said to the woman, "Did God really say, 'You must not eat from any tree in the garden'?" The woman said to the serpent, "We may eat fruit from the trees in the garden, but God did say, 'You must not eat fruit from the tree that is in the middle of the garden, and you must not touch it, or you will die.' You will not surely die," the serpent said to the woman. "For God knows that when you eat of it your eyes will be opened, and you will be like God, knowing good and evil." When the woman saw that the fruit of the tree was good for food and pleasing to the eye, and also desirable for gaining wisdom, she took some and

> ate it. She also gave some to her husband,
> who was with her, and he ate it. Then the eyes
> of both of them were opened.
>
> —GENESIS 3:1–7

Satan's goal then and ever since has been to disrupt the close, loving, and trusting relationship with God we were designed for. The devil wants to twist the truth and divert us—as he did our original parents, Adam and Eve—into eternal separation from our Creator.

It worked, too. Because of that original sin and the flood of sins humanity has committed in the millennia since the Garden of Eden, we are—without Christ and the unmerited favor, grace, and forgiveness provided by the Son of God's sacrifice on the cross—in dis-fellowship with the Lord of life.

When you realize the depths of mankind's hopeless fate without Christ, indeed, the dark spiritual destination that awaits your own lost family members if they enter eternity without embracing God's forgiveness, you *must* act. And when you do, by sending a steady stream of intercessory prayer for those sons, daughters, parents, and others to the throne of God, don't expect the enemy to take it lying down.

Expect the devil to rise up against you. He and his legions of demons will attack and do all they can to discourage you, to make you give up, and to distract you from your mission of seeing your loved ones in the arms of Jesus. Any setback, sickness, or series of hurtful words coming at you from unexpected sources—even those same lost family members you are trying to lead to Christ—*will* come with a spirit of discouragement.

You might have started this journey of holding up your lost relatives to God for salvation many years ago, but then you found yourself backing away from that initial determination after being worn down by demonic counterattacks.

Here's another question for you to mull over. Let's say I have two children, and let's say you have two children of your own; none of them know Christ. (I am thankful that in reality my own son and daughter do serve the Lord, but this is for the sake of making a point, OK?)

So, imagine if God then said to me, "Arni, you can have your two children come to Christ, or these other two be saved. Decide which will be in heaven with me and which will go to hell." Of course, God would never make such a demand, but, for the purpose of this illustration, what if He did?

Like any human parent, I would choose my own two kids in a heartbeat. I don't want my children to go to hell, or any of my blood relatives to end up in that place of never-ending torment, regret, and separation from all that is good—all that is God.

Let me stop briefly here to address a disturbing trend I've seen among God's people in recent years: downplaying, even ignoring the reality of hell. I need to state this as clearly as possible: hell is a real place.

In fact, I think some of us need a fresh vision of hell. In his book *23 Minutes in Hell*, Bill Wiese writes about an out-of-body experience during which he believes Jesus took him on a terrifying tour of hell.[1] The purpose was for him to testify about the reality of this place to an increasingly complacent world that would rather play it down or completely write it off as make-believe, boogeyman stuff invented to keep us in line.

His book has become a best seller, and Bill is a sought-after speaker on this subject. However, he says that making money from his experience was not the motivation for writing the book. He was doing fine as a successful Southern California real estate agent, but he felt compelled by his terrifying tour of Satan's realm to share the truth.

Unbearable heat, flames, and yet impenetrable darkness; isolation and regret; agony and hopelessness; multiplied by an existence of pain and unfathomable fear amid Satan and his hate-filled minions—that is the hell described in great detail by *23 Minutes in Hell*. But Weiss also stresses the compassion of Christ, Bill's guide on this soul-wrenching journey.

Bill wrote that Jesus made it clear to him that not only does our heavenly Father see our tears for those risking an eternity without His forgiveness and grace, but His own tears would fill an ocean without shores big enough to contain them.

Hell was never meant for God's human children. We are creations made in His image and were brought to life with His own breath of Spirit. No, hell was reserved for Satan and his rebellious angels, and God held back nothing—not even his own Son, who stepped into time and space to live, teach, die on the cross, and rise again—to ransom us from the consequences of our own sins.

"The reason I was shown this was to bring back a message of warning," Bill wrote. "My story is not one to condemn, but rather to inform you that hell is a real place—it does exist. God's desire is that no one goes there. But the sad and simple fact is that people make the choice to go to hell every day."[2]

That does not mean God will not do all He can to woo those lost loved ones to His enormous, forgiving heart. For that, throughout human history, He has offered a straightforward contract of compassion: *His covenant.*

God wants you to know this: This Acts 16 covenant is an unshakable, undeniable, ironclad contract signed, sealed, and, through faith, delivered in heaven itself. It is His chosen means to release all His limitless power to bring those precious to you to the point of their own decision—fully aware, their vision clear of Satan's deception and diversions. He wants all of us to embrace Jesus as our personal Savior.

So, yes, hell is real. Jesus warned about it time and again during His ministry on Earth. Fifteen times He discussed hell in the Gospels and once more in the Book of Revelation, where He appeared to the apostle John. In the Gospel of Luke, Christ preached about hell in the parable of the rich man and the beggar Lazarus.

Jesus told of the self-indulgence and extravagant lifestyle of the rich man; he wore the best clothes, his meals were lavish banquets—in short, his days were spent in luxury. However, just a short distance from the rich man's table, at the very gate leading into his estate, was Lazarus. Scripture describes this destitute man as "covered with sores and longing to eat what fell from the rich man's table. Even the dogs came and licked his sores" (Luke 16:20–21).

OK, let me put this in the Arni version: Lazarus was a bum. And as things turned out, the bum and the rich man croaked at the same time. Lazarus, who had suffered so much on Earth, goes to heaven. He even has an escort of angels. The rich man headed south—way south, to hell.

> He was in torment, he looked up and saw Abraham far away, with Lazarus by his side. So he called to him, "Father Abraham, have pity on me and send Lazarus to dip the tip of his finger in water and cool my tongue, because I am in agony in this fire." But Abraham replied, "Son, remember that in your lifetime you received your good things, while Lazarus received bad things, but now he is comforted here and you are in agony. And besides all this, between us and you a great chasm has been fixed, so that those who want to go from here to you cannot, nor can anyone cross over from there to us."
>
> —LUKE 16:23–26

The rich man, his own hopes dashed, still loved his family, though. And even from hell, he begged them to escape from his own fate.

> "Father, send Lazarus to my father's house, for I have five brothers. Let him warn them, so that they will not also come to this place of torment.... If someone from the dead goes to them, they will repent."
>
> —LUKE 16:27, 30

The request was denied. The rich man may or may not have someday seen more of his family join him in torment. Abraham made it clear that would be up to them—and the extent to which they heeded the warnings given to them in Scripture and prophecy.

That's the simple truth. When they die, your brother, your sister, your mom and dad, your relatives who don't know Christ are going to hell. It doesn't sound nice, but it is the truth. That's the Bible, not Arni Jacobson. This sobering biblical truth drives me, and it should spur you on, too.

It is in the here and now that our loved ones must be reached. This is all-out war between the saints of God and Satan.

Militant, you say? Yes, it is! We need to be serious—to be militant—about fighting for our sons, daughters, siblings, parents, aunts, uncles, cousins, and others we care about. We need to embrace, not yawn, at the old gospel chorus, "Onward Christian soldiers, marching as to war, with the cross of Jesus going on before."

So, pray and enlist new recruits to be prayer warriors in the cause of your loved ones. Get on the front lines and expect a battle. And remember, we are on the winning team. Read all about it in the last chapters of the Bible!

Never give up. *Never.* God doesn't; neither should you.

Points to remember

- Stand strong against Satan and expect demonic opposition.

- Hell is a real place, and God wants none of us to go there.

- God has a covenant with you to bring your family to the cross.

CHAPTER 3

KEY NO. 3

EXPECT AN UPROAR IN YOUR FAMILY

FOLLOWING THE ACTS 16 adventures of Paul and Silas in Philippi, we learned of the uproar that resulted when satanic influences, operating through the lies of the men who had lost the services of a fortune-telling slave girl freed from demon possession when Paul booted the devil out in Jesus' name.

This is where we discover key number three and this warning: when you get serious about praying for the salvation for those wayward family members, be ready for the uproar. And when your loved ones begin to come to Christ—and they will when you begin to apply these keys to get the engine of God's promise started—all hell will break loose. That uproar *will* begin, and it will come from among the unsaved in your family. I know; I've lived it, and to some extent I still do!

In the introduction to this book, I told you how I owed my salvation to my sister, Judy. It is a story that I first shared fully in *Favor Factor*. I won't repeat the entire thing here, but a couple points can be applied to the number three key we're talking about.

Judy's becoming born again caused an uproar in our family. And though I tell you today that her changed life paved the way for me to accept Christ, it took more than three years for the Holy Spirit to bring me to that point. It was several months after Judy died before I prayed the sinner's prayer with Pastor Wilkerson in that restaurant.

Before I took that step, my brother and parents had accepted Christ. As more family members came to the Lord, those who remained unsaved—and I was among them—greeted the conversions with feelings ranging from amusement over these new evangelical "born-agains" to jealousy of their new peace and happiness. There was even outright anger over the conviction our sinful lifestyles brought when we compared them to the changed lives of the recently saved relatives.

When I became one of those born-agains, the same reactions targeted me, the salesman-turned-preacher. A friend of mine from high school offered this judgment: "Arni, they have brainwashed you." I replied, "Yes, Dick. I had a dirty old brain that needed a good old washing!"

Others had this to say: "Those churches just want your money," or, "How could you leave the denomination you were raised in for these holy-rollers?"

But always, and I bet it is this way with you, too, those on the outside criticizing your decision to follow Christ focus on the money. Man, they hear about tithing and it's, "Ah, they just want your dough." They just don't understand. I told one of my relatives after I was saved, "Yeah, I'm giving 10 percent to tithing. But I used to give 70 percent to the taverns, so I figure I'm still 60 percent up!"

As a pastor, I've never backed away from preaching about giving what the Bible calls those "first fruits" to God's work as a tithe on your income. I don't apologize for it. If you live up to what you know is right and do things God's way, He has made a promise that every one of those family members will come to Christ before they die. Being faithful in your lifestyle, prayer, worship, and yes, tithing is part of the package.

Now, I'd like nothing better than to have God take out a heavenly chainsaw, cut a hole in the church roof, and drop a big chunk of gold bullion down. Imagine needing a truck to haul that away to the bank? All our money needs would be met with the price of gold being what it is today.

But to God, who certainly could do that (well, probably not with a chainsaw), it's the principles behind tithing that matter. He wants His people to participate in provision for the church and its work, to sacrifice a little, to remember where their blessings come from in the first place.

OK, on from that mini-sermon and back to "the uproar factor." The reaction I'm talking about also surprised Bill and Mary, a couple who came to visit our church in Green Bay, Wisconsin. Bill and Mary loved the worship service, and both answered the call to invite Christ into their lives. They had three small children who thrived in our kids' ministry programs, and the whole family was baptized and joined our church.

The resulting uproar in their family stunned even me. Mary had been raised in a strong Roman Catholic family, and her mother was of the belief that if you weren't Catholic, you were damned. Mary's mom was sincere in her beliefs but of course wrong in so limiting membership in the family of God. She was also wrong in the course of action she then pursued.

Suddenly, the mother banned not only her daughter but her own grandchildren from visiting. Mary's father was heartbroken; he had embraced a personal relationship with Christ while remaining within the Catholic Church. And, let's be clear, Christ's gift is no respecter of denominations. Still, the mother's opposition created a painful rift in Mary's family.

While deeply hurt, Mary and Bill remained strong in their new walk with Christ, and their faith was to be rewarded in a unique way.

Green Bay then was a city of only about one hundred thousand, but its fame was worldwide as the home of professional football's Green Bay Packers. Without the team, I often joke, Green Bay would be just another Fargo, North Dakota. (That's not to say that Fargo, to its inhabitants, isn't a fine place to live, OK? But you get the idea.)

Mary's parents, as it happened, were big-time Packers fans. They were especially fond of the player who wore the number sixty-six jersey, Ray Nitschke, the NFL's all-time leading linebacker. I had the joy of leading Ray and his wife to Christ, and in 1998 he died of a heart attack. I had the honor of officiating his funeral, which included much about the change the Lord had brought in his life.

That afternoon, Mary's dad called and invited his daughter and family to visit. Surprised the ban had apparently been lifted, they rushed over. Mary's mom, it turned out, had watched the funeral on TV, as it had been broadcast from our church.

"I can see now why you attend that church," she told Mary. The rift, finally, was being healed.

The point is that yes, there had been an uproar within Mary's family as a result of them becoming born again. But as always, God came through.

The Bible promises that "everyone who wants to live a godly life in Christ Jesus will be persecuted, while evil men and impostors will go from bad to worse, deceiving and being deceived" (2 Tim. 3:12–13).

The Message puts the same passage this way:

> Anyone who wants to live all out for Christ is in for a lot of trouble; there's no getting around it. Unscrupulous con men will continue to exploit the faith. They're as deceived as the people they lead astray. As long as they are out there, things can only get worse.

Oh, yes, the uproar that follows inevitably when we devote our lives—and prayers for the salvation of our loved ones—to the Lord will hurt. Especially, those hurtful words you hear to your face, and particularly those you hear about after the ridicule and derision is spoken behind your back, will tear at your heart.

"Sticks and stones may break my bones, but words will never hurt me." That old saying is a lie from the pit of hell, as far as I'm concerned. I know I'd rather exchange a punch in the nose for the hurtful words I've heard from some.

But *never* give up. Give those hurts to Jesus to handle, and drive on.

Paul and Silas, though bloody, bruised, and locked in the stocks amid the filth and criminal company of that Philippian prison, didn't give up. Not only that, but the Bible tells us they held a midnight worship service! They were hardly in a nice, warm, and carpeted church auditorium, wearing their Sunday finest and sitting in padded pews; they were praying and singing hymns, inhaling lungs-full of putrid air. This was a strange occurrence. Their fellow prisoners were listening, perhaps in admiration mixed with amazement. Or, maybe they just thought they were enjoying a crazy show. But they listened.

Paul and Silas had been jailed for creating an uproar, by false accusations and demonic opposition. Now, it was God's turn, and this heavenly uproar would make the devil's effort look like amateur hour.

> Suddenly there was such a violent earthquake that the foundations of the prison were shaken. At once all the prison doors flew open, and everybody's chains came loose. The jailer woke up, and when he saw the prison doors open, he drew his sword and was about to kill himself because he thought the prisoners had escaped.
>
> —ACTS 16:26–27

The officer in charge of the prison had good reason to consider suicide instead of what awaited him for allowing any escapes. Under the Romans' practice, a jailer who allowed a prisoner to escape would suffer the same penalty the missing inmate was due. Considering this was the prison's cell for its worst offenders, that likely meant flogging and execution. In other words, a quick thrust of the sword in the right place would be a lot less painful, and quicker.

But God had other plans for this particular jailer. Acts 16:28 tells us that "Paul shouted, 'Don't harm yourself! We are all here!'" Or as *The Message* puts it, "Paul stopped him: 'Don't do that! We're all still here! Nobody's run away!'"

Another part of this midnight miracle in old Philippi was that very fact that none of these desperadoes had beat feet out of there the first chance they had. The jailer called for torches so he could see for himself; all the vermin were there, along with Paul and Silas. He was astounded, grateful, and—realizing something supernatural was afoot— terrified. He fell at Paul's feet, trembling.

"Sirs, what must I do to be saved?" he asked (Acts 16:30). Now the jailer was thinking of more than his brief mortal life, of relationship with the kind of God who could do such things as he had just witnessed.

Paul responded, "Believe in the Lord Jesus, and you will be saved—you and your household" (v. 31).

That part of the story always gets me. Let's say you're in that prison for knocking off the First Bank of Rome. In the process you shot an arrow through the heart of the teller, and you're sentenced to death. Then, *wham*, earthquake, doors open. Are you going to stick around to hear these guys sing their next tune? Not me. I'm out of there!

But you stay. It's a miracle, part two. The anointing in that place is so strong you just can't move.

Uproar. Foiled again, Satan. The enemy sought to end the gospel's growth in a place called Philippi, even managing to get Paul and Silas in the ancient world's equivalent of death row. God intervened and saved not only them but also the jailer and his whole family when they accepted Christ and were baptized that very night.

While you and I may indeed someday be imprisoned for our faith, the truth is that today the uproar we create when we go to prayer for our unsaved loved ones will come in other forms. But even feeling like we have been stripped naked and beaten by the stinging whips of our relatives' tongues is no fun.

Too many Christians simply quit at this point. They are overwhelmed by the uproar triggered by their prayers and testimony within the family. But never give up. Victory is coming!

Some points to remember

- Expect an uproar from unsaved family members.

- Being faithful in your lifestyle, prayer, worship, and tithing is part of the package.

- Words do hurt. Give them to the Lord and drive on.

CHAPTER 4

KEY NO. 4

CREATE AN ENVIRONMENT OF WORSHIP TO BUILD YOUR BOLDNESS

REMEMBER HOW PAUL AND Silas were in stocks, lying in the filth of the Philippian jail's high-security cell praying and singing? You may ask, How in the world could they do that, their bruised and bleeding bodies throbbing with pain, and all the while knowing that, humanly, their chances of getting out of their predicament alive were slim to none?

The answer is that from the depths of their hearts and spirits, they knew the truth of our fourth key: spiritual worship is a strong force in evangelism, both for Christian men and women and for those lost loved ones of yours.

I love to worship God. The Holy Spirit has shown me that worship is one of the strongest tools available to believers fighting for souls on the front lines of our war against Satan. It is more than a strong characteristic of growing churches throughout the world today, too.

Yet, how many times have you ever said, "I'm just too tired today to worship;" or, "I'm too sick today to worship;" or even, "I just don't feel like worshiping." Baloney. Those are exactly the times you should be hitting it hardest.

Worship can give you the faith for that cantankerous aunt or uncle or son or daughter or whomever it is in your family who needs Christ. If you have the right heart when you come before God, worship can open up the blessings. As you praise God, visualize your family getting saved, and you are sharing that hope and confidence on a new, deeper level with the Lord.

Excuses not to worship? Paul and Silas could have made them in spades. Consider the day they had. They were hounded by a demon-possessed girl, arrested under false charges, beaten by a mob, flogged, and tossed into a dungeon with the expectation of a death sentence.

Humanly speaking, I think they had far more claim to excuses for not worshiping God than any of us. You or I probably would just whine, "That's it. I'm checking out. This is just too tough."

But faced with an apparent dead-end to their ministry, Paul and Silas knew the tool to use for a breakout—not necessarily from prison, though it did have that eventual effect. The breaking point was worship; that is what triggered the miraculous events that saved them and brought a jailer and his family to Christ.

I'll come back to this shortly. There is a story from the Old Testament that is instructive here, too, when it comes to the power of worship in blowing away the roadblocks Satan and his minions try to throw in our way. Grab your Bible and turn to Isaiah 6. Let's explore this together.

> In the year that King Uzziah died, I saw the Lord seated on a throne, high and exalted, and the train of his robe filled the temple. Above him were seraphs, each with six wings: With two wings they covered their faces, with two they covered their feet, and with two they were flying. And they were calling to one another: "Holy, holy, holy is the Lord Almighty; the whole earth is full of his glory." At the sound of their voices the doorposts and thresholds shook and the temple was filled with smoke. "Woe to me!" I cried. "I am ruined! For I am a man of unclean lips, and I live among a people of unclean lips, and my eyes have seen the King, the Lord Almighty." Then one of the seraphs flew to me with a live coal in his hand, which he had taken with tongs from the altar. With it he touched my mouth and said, "See,

this has touched your lips; your guilt is taken
away and your sin atoned for." Then I heard
the voice of the Lord saying, "Whom shall I
send? And who will go for us?" And I said,
"Here am I. Send me!"

—Isaiah 6:1–8

When Isaiah came to the temple in Jerusalem
on that day in 740 B.C., he was in mourning. King
Uzziah was his cousin, and "Uz" (good nickname,
I figure) generally had been a good and godly ruler.
However, he grew too proud of himself. He burned
his own incense in the temple, committing a serious
sin by usurping the God-designated role of the
consecrated high priests. They tried to stop him, but
he angrily pushed them aside and lit up anyway.

As he continued to rage at the priests who had
tried to save him from his own rebellion, leprosy
broke out on his forehead. The same flesh-eating
disease eventually killed him. Even his burial
place—in a field near the royal tombs but not within
that hallowed site—was a sad reminder of God's
judgment.

All of these things, along with the love Isaiah
felt for his blood relative's fate, must have been
going through the prophet's mind as he went to
the temple that day looking for comfort and direction from his God. And he got it in overwhelming,

life-changing, soul-shaking measure that would be worth recording for the ages.

What Isaiah walked into was an awesome worship service! Through visionary eyes, he saw the Ancient of Days on his throne, the very train, or hem, of His robes filling the temple—symbolic, some Jewish scholars believe, of how God's power fills the physical as well as spiritual world. A variety of angelic beings were flying around, filling Isaiah's ears with words of praise to the King of the universe.

As Psalm 148:2 tells us, angels were created long before human beings, and for the purpose of worshiping God: "Praise him, all his angels, praise him, all his heavenly hosts." A similar take comes in the New Testament: "But you have come to Mount Zion, to the heavenly Jerusalem, the city of the living God. You have come to thousands upon thousands of angels in joyful assembly" (Heb. 12:22).

You can see it would be an enormous mistake to underestimate the value of worship to God!

Realizing how far he, a mere man, fell short of being worthy to witness such holiness, Isaiah lamented that he was completely unworthy. Even as a prophet of God, he knew he was still a member of the human race and a rebellious people. God's answer, symbolized by a live coal from the altar inside the temple's inner most holy place, was forgiveness;

an angel touched the coal to Isaiah's "unclean lips" and declared him guiltless before God.

Declared worthy of the Lord's love through a pure act of grace, Isaiah joyfully embraced his new purpose to warn the people of Israel of the consequences of their sin. This all came about within an atmosphere of worship. Worship, it seems clear, is the critical ingredient to unleashing the power and purpose of the Lord in our lives!

Now, back to that Philippian prison. That midnight worship service led by Paul and Silas was no less an anointed event than what Isaiah recorded. The worst of the worst criminals were with them in that inner cell, and yet they listened to the prayers and hymns. I think that the presence of God had burrowed beneath layers of evil deeds eventually to touch their hearts.

No matter the place—a prison or a megachurch—you will be touched by the power of worship.

Many of you reading this book have tried sharing Christ with your family, only to endure rejection. Don't give up! Worship instead, and see the Holy Spirit work in you, and in the lives of your lost loved ones, in awesome ways.

When the uproar from within your family comes—and expect it to come—don't give up.

- Continue to *pray* for those loved ones daily.

- Continue to *stand* strong against Satan.

- Continue to *expect* that exciting uproar within your family.

- And continue to *create* an environment of worship to build your boldness.

God's promise, His *covenant* with you, is to bless and empower your mission to bring your family to a clear point of decision for Christ. The Lord wants to prepare their hearts to openly hear the message of salvation and reconciliation.

Worship will put you in lockstep with the power and purpose of the Lord, and like Paul and Silas learned, that is when the miracles begin. Expect something marvelous to come for you and your family. Perhaps it will even be the equivalent of a spiritual earthquake.

Some points to remember

- Worship unleashes God peace, power, and purpose.

- Worship clears away spiritual barriers.

- Expect something marvelous, a spiritual earthquake in your family!

CHAPTER 5

KEY NO. 5

BELIEVE FROM THE DEPTHS OF YOUR HEART YOUR FAMILY WILL COME TO CHRIST

W E LAST LEFT THAT Philippian prison master on his knees before Paul and Silas, saved from suicide and asking them for the way to salvation. Remember the answer? "Believe in the Lord Jesus, and you will be saved—you and your household" (Acts 16:31).

Do you have doubts that these guys were talking about lost family members? *Household*? Try leading your three-bedroom, two-bath house with the two-car garage and landscaped backyard to the Lord. Even try leading your carpet, sheet rock, or furniture to Christ. It doesn't work. So, yes, *household* means your lost loved ones! (OK, that was some corny humor, I know, but I just wanted to be clear.)

Anyway, the jailer accepted Christ, and when all those in his house—where he took Paul and Silas to have their wounds bathed and to be fed a good meal—heard the message, the rest of the family got saved, too. In fact, the whole bunch was dunked into their new faith that very morning: "Immediately he and all his family were baptized" (Acts 16:33).

This is God's covenant with us at work. It is just like that old children's chorus many of you may have sung in Sunday school:

> Every promise in the Book is mine
> Every chapter every verse, every line
> All the blessings of His love divine,
> Every promise in the Book is mine.

I mentioned the importance of the covenant concept earlier in brief. But it is important for you to realize that point in more depth. So, let's take another moment to explore that; I want to be sure it is embedded at the core of your very soul, at the foundation of your faith. It is a critical keystone to this final key of believing from the depths of your heart your family will come to Christ.

The Hebrew word translated in the Old Testament as "covenant" is *berith*. At its root meaning, *berith* recalls the ancient practice of sealing a solemn agreement by literally passing between the severed parts of a slaughtered, sacrificial animal. Abraham's vision, recounted in Genesis 15, was of a smoking fire pot and a blazing torch—symbolic of God's presence—passing between those pieces. Then, the Lord declared His vow to give the Promised Land of Israel to Abraham's descendants.

In the New Testament, the Greek word translated as "covenant" is *diatheke*. It, too, refers to an unbreakable agreement, similar to a will or testament. It is an irrevocable decision, one that cannot be canceled by anyone.

Thus the origin of the term *New Testament*, as we call the four Gospels, the Book of Acts, the epistles to the early church, and the Book of Revelation. But first and foremost, the New Testament is God's pact of grace and reconciliation, this time through the blood of His own Son, as Jesus explained at the Last Supper:

> And he took bread, gave thanks and broke it, and gave it to them, saying, "This is my body given for you; do this in remembrance of me." In the same way, after the supper he took the cup, saying, "This cup is the new covenant in my blood, which is poured out for you."
>
> —LUKE 22:19–20

The Message uses these words for that passage: "'This is my body, given for you. Eat it in my memory.' He did the same with the cup after supper, saying, 'This cup is the new covenant written in my blood, blood poured out for you.'"

Finally, in case you may have missed this idea up to now, you can rely completely on God's promises—and the statement in Acts 16:31 is a promise!

What does the Bible say about God's promises?

> God is not a man, that he should lie, nor a son of man, that he should change his mind. Does he speak and then not act? Does he promise and not fulfill?
>
> —Numbers 23:19

"Believe in the Lord Jesus, and you will be saved— you and your household" (Acts 16:31). God has promised us He will withhold nothing of His power to bring your family members to a saving knowledge of His Son. It is His covenant to us, sealed in the blood of His own precious Son.

Visualize this covenant, this New Testament, as a real document. See a scroll, signed in holy blood, and God sliding it across the table to you.

That's right, the kind of covenant we're discussing here is a two-way agreement. The Bible makes that very clear. Consider these kinds of "conditional" covenants God offered and how their fulfillment rode on the extent of man's honoring their terms.

An old, dying man, David had warned Solomon to "walk in [God's] ways, and keep his decrees and commands...that the Lord may keep his promise to me" concerning future generations of kingly descent (1 Kings 2:3–4). When Solomon eventually broke this agreement by worshiping and sacrificing to other gods, the results were catastrophic. The kingdom was split, leaving the coming generations of Davidic kings with just two of the twelve tribes of Israel to rule.

So, yes, you have a part to play in opening the floodgates of God's love, mercy, and irresistible courtship of that son, daughter, father or mother, brother or sister, niece or nephew, or cousin now so distant from Christ's blessings in this life and the life to come.

The five keys to seeing the Acts 16:31 promises come to reality are contained in this book. They are not mine; they are the Lord's, clearly taught in Scripture. And they are the essential ingredients to fulfilling our part of this covenant God has offered His children through the ministry in Philippi of Paul and Silas.

The keys, then, are like a blueprint from the Architect. Blueprints are carefully crafted in exact and complete detail in order for the contractors and workers to have a clear, step-by-step process to making a dream into concrete reality. And, like any bricklayer, pipefitter, welder, or drywaller, we need tools to help us do our part.

Ready to get to work? Are you ready to:

- *pray* every day for your unsaved family members?

- *stand* strong against Satan?

- *expect* an exciting uproar in your family?

- And, are you ready to *believe* from the depths of your heart that your family will come to Christ?

Time to get acquainted with your spiritual tool chest.

Points to remember

- The Acts 16:31 promise is God's covenant with us for our families.

- Visualize God's contract, signed in Christ's blood.

He just slid the covenant scroll over to
you; will you sign it?

CHAPTER 6

YOUR FIVE KEYS SPIRITUAL TOOL CHEST

WHAT FOLLOWS IN THIS final chapter are a couple helpful tools and suggestions for how to kick-start your Five Keys journey.

But by way of reintroducing those keys to you, I want to reemphasize the first: Pray every day for your unsaved family members.

Prayer is praise, and prayer is communion. Prayer allows your heart to listen to God's direction and to receive the Lord's peace and confidence in your endeavors to lead your loved ones to Christ.

The more you get to know Him, the closer you get.

As I write this, I have been married to my wife, Jan, for forty-two years. That's a lot of communion! And during that time, we have gotten to know each other very well, indeed. We can finish each other's sentences, share each other's thoughts. We can be sitting in our family room and I'll bring up something, and, inevitably, she will respond, "I was just thinking about that very thing." I know what she likes; she knows what I like.

We should also get to that point of spiritual intimacy with God. He already, of course, knows what we like—and we should strive to return at least a fragment of that understanding about His desires for us and our families.

In this way, prayer becomes a lifestyle. But so many times, what we give God is our leftover time, after a busy, stressful day. I urge you to give God the best part of your day for prayer, first thing in the morning, before your mind and heart are distracted by everyday life.

Earlier in this book, I told you about the amazing ministry of Korean pastor David Yonggi *Cho*, and how prayer had literally fueled the growth of what is today the world's largest single evangelical Christian church. What you don't know, perhaps, is that Cho learned the key of prayer from his mother-in-law.

This godly and insistent woman would rise at 4:30 a.m. and pound on her son-in-law's door. "Time to pray, David!" she would firmly remind him. It was a lesson he passed on to his own family and to the hundreds of thousands of Koreans who were won to Christ through his ministry.

So, first you pray. Then you stand strong against Satan when the counterattacks come. Opposition also will come from within your own family, so expect an exciting uproar among those unsaved loved ones. Be prepared for hurtful reactions. But you don't give up! You get the strength to persevere by creating an environment of worship, not forgetting that you must believe from the depths of your heart that your family will come to Christ.

To underscore your commitment to the Five Keys, you might consider writing a letter to those you will be praying for, like my good friend Michael in Green Bay, Wisconsin, did.

Michael wrote this letter after his sister, brother-in-law and nephew tragically died. He has given me permission to quote portions of that letter with you here.

To my Family, Friends and Associates:

In the last year and a half it appears to me that time is passing at a very fast pace. With the passing of Nancy, Richard and Michael....I find myself looking at life differently. The times we are living in, the direction our country is taking, the ungodly leadership that's in power, having no moral compass, [has me] concerned for our children and grandchildren.

I believe I have been given much in many areas of life. I believe I have a responsibility to share what has been given to me. Luke 12:48: "For everyone to whom much is given, from him much will be required" [NKJV].

I am recognizing the fact that.... "Whereas ye know not what shall be on the morrow. For what is your life? It is even a vapour, that appeareth for a little time, and then vanisheth away" [James 4:14, KJV].

My heart has been moved to write this letter to you to let you know that I don't want any more time to go by without sharing what I believe are some of the most important things in life.... this letter is not written to condemn anyone [but] this letter may bring conviction. Conviction brings hope for a positive change in your life. Condemnation brings fear, anger and hopelessness.

If I could give you one precious piece of advice [it] is that God loves you and has a plan for you. Jeremiah 29:11–14 (*The Message* Bible): "I know what I'm doing. I have it all planned out—plans to take care of you, not abandon you, plans to give you the future you hope for. When you call on me, when you come and pray to me, I'll listen. When you come looking for me, you'll find me. Yes, when you get serious about finding

me and want it more than anything else, I'll
make sure you won't be disappointed. God's
Decree. I'll turn things around for you."

Michael concludes by telling his letter's recipi-
ents, "I know that God loves me and I want you to
have the same assurance."

Such a letter, in your own words, could be one of
the tools you can use to get started.

To that, I add my own suggestion: make a list,
what I call a strategy card. It should include a listing
of the keys discussed in this book and have space
for the names of lost loved ones, the date you began
praying for them, and the date on which they are
saved. (I'm including a template of this for you at
the end of this chapter.)

It is God's promise to you—His covenant—that
He holds His family in His hands and loves them
more deeply than you or I can fathom. Follow the
Five Keys, and let's agree that we will see all of your
family members won into the kingdom of our Lord
and Savior, Jesus Christ!

Points to remember

- ⊶ Prayer is praise; prayer is communion.

- ⊶ Make prayer a lifestyle, giving God the best part of your day.

- ⊶ Make a list of those you are praying for and track their salvation journeys.

FIVE KEYS TO REACHING YOUR FAMILY FOR CHRIST STRATEGY CARD

ACTS 16:16–32

- Pray every day for your unsaved family members.
- Stand strong against Satan.
- Expect an exciting uproar in your family.
- Create an environment of worship to build your boldness.
- Believe from the depths of your heart that your family will come to Christ.

	Name	Today's Date	Date Saved
1.			
2.			
3.			
4			
5.			

Remember: Don't ever give up. God hasn't; neither should you!

MORE
ENCOURAGEMENT
FOR THE JOURNEY

HERE ARE SOME FINAL encouraging examples of the power of prayer, faith, and persistence in leading loved ones to Christ.

THE STORY OF MARK STANICH:
A LONG ROAD HOME

From almost the beginning of Mark Stanich's life, he was in trouble. By the time he was two years old, he was already in full rebellion. He was a stubborn, strong-willed boy with a raging temper who would react to discipline by banging his head against the wall.

Life itself seemed to conspire against Mark at times. At five years old, while walking home from kindergarten with his six-year-old brother Michael, Mark was struck by a car. The already troubled boy suffered a broken arm and leg, cracked ribs, and bruised kidneys—and, a doctor would later surmise, brain damage. Mark spent six weeks in traction and then went home in a body cast he wore for another month and a half.

His accident resulted in Mark having one leg two inches shorter than the other, a painfully curved spine, and the need for later corrective surgery. By the second grade, Mark was having trouble keeping up in school, and at the same time he was choosing to take risks that resulted in multiple injuries and returns to the emergency room. By age nine, he was secretly smoking; at age thirteen, he was drinking.

Neither the teachings of his Christian parents, Doug and Joan, nor the influence of their Bible-believing church (where the Staniches regularly attended, tithed, and served) seemed to dent Mark's sad and angry start to life. At fourteen, church youth leaders learned Mark was using marijuana; a year later, he stole his brother Michael's car and was arrested after running a stop sign and for driving without a license.

Mark, who already had been skipping classes, quit going to school altogether and ran away to live with a friend. By sixteen, he had fathered a child out of wedlock, something he denied until DNA tests proved paternity.

It only got worse from there. He was in multiple car accidents while driving drunk or under the influence of drugs. He married and divorced three times, fathering children with two of those wives. He built a criminal record that included domestic violence, and during one incident Doug had to talk Mark into surrendering to a SWAT team.

Doug and Joan footed the bill for Mark's behavior repeatedly, including six attempts at drug and alcohol rehabilitation. Finally, they had to kick him out of their home. He roamed from one job to another, mostly in sales positions, where he would woo customers with his good looks, charisma, and sense of humor, only to take advantage of them and further soil his reputation.

At age thirty-eight, Mark was again in trouble with the law, dodging an arrest warrant and threatening suicide rather than surrender. Police arrested him at a hospital, where he spent time in a psychiatric unit, then was taken to jail. Most of Mark's final four years of life were spent behind bars on various charges, the most serious involving his forging of a prescription for the powerful painkiller OxyContin.

But having hit bottom in a Wisconsin prison, a miracle happened. For decades, Doug and Joan had prayed for their son's salvation. Despite the agony of seemingly unanswered prayers and the unending hurt of his actions, Mark's parents never gave up on him.

In prison, his life in shambles, Mark turned to the Lord and began reading the Bible. He witnessed to other inmates, and when he was finally released in September 2005, his parents provided him with a job, a truck, housing, and support for his attempt to start over. Once again, though, Doug and Joan saw the signs that Mark was losing ground.

"It became evident within a few weeks that he was drug seeking and reverting back to old habits," Doug recalls. "But before he could fall again, we believe God intervened."

One morning Joan received a call from the police, who had found Mark dead in his Kenosha, Wisconsin, apartment. She and Doug met at the scene, finding their son sitting upright, a look of peace on his still face, his body still warm. The cause of death was listed as a heart attack.

In the coming days and weeks, the grieving Stanich family learned that in Mark's last days, he had truly surrendered his life to Christ. One friend told of conversations where happiness and love had finally seemed to replace a lifetime of anger and selfishness.

"He had spent much time praying, and he was convinced that God was going to take care of him," the friend told them. "It was obvious he was at peace with himself and with God."

Doug and Joan, though they had to bury Mark just six weeks after his release from prison, also had peace. God had answered their prayer; they will see their boy again in heaven.

A "PHOTOGRAPH" OF FAMILY SALVATION

My friend Brian Gowan has a vision for evangelism and serving the emotionally, physically, and spiritually downtrodden as pastor of Community Transformation for Grace Community Church in Houston, Texas. His decades of ministry have immersed him and his family in reaching out to the homeless, the sick, the forgotten seniors in nursing homes, and those suffering amid inner-city poverty.

But Brian says his first, and lifelong, call to evangelism has been his own extended family. Shortly after he accepted Christ as a high school senior in 1973, the Holy Spirit lovingly but firmly put the salvation of his loved ones at the core of his heart.

"I remember experiencing an unusual combination of unspeakable joy—and grief," Brian says. "The joy was for being and feeling personally forgiven.

But the waves of grief overcame me as I meditated on the *lostness* not just of the entire world, but of my immediate family."

God wasted little time giving Brian's prayer answers. Within a week of his own acceptance of Christ, Brian saw one of his brothers, John, come to a miraculous, living room encounter with the Lord. "The presence of God came down and literally hit us like a tangible electric force, so much so that we could hardly keep hanging on to each others' hands as we joined in prayer," Brian recounts.

Next up was Brian's oldest brother, Gary, the cynic of the family. It took longer, but over time Brian's prayerful intercession for his big brother, despite frequent arguments and apparent setbacks, were answered. Gary accepted Christ, married a Christian woman, and has been serving the Lord ever since—more than thirty years now.

A sister, Carolyn, was the next to embrace Christ, after years more of Brian's prayers and patient testimony. Eventually, all five of Brian's siblings became born again believers—even joined by their mother.

Recently, Brian, his wife, and their two children went to a family reunion in the Pacific Northwest. As is typical of such gatherings, lots of pictures were taken to celebrate the time together. When the reunion was over, Brian and his brood returned to Houston.

Some time later, they picked up the developed pictures from the reunion. Brian looked at one group shot of his extended family, anchored by his mother, seated in the center of the photograph.

"As I carefully gazed on the scene, I examined each face, from my grandmother's to that of the youngest child. With my finger, I counted them, touching each person and saying, 'In Christ…in Christ…in Christ…' To my utter amazement and joy, all thirty-four of them in that reunion photograph had experienced a personal encounter and salvation experience with Jesus Christ!"

In 2008, Brian's mother passed away at age eighty-six. She had been among the first of his family to join him in serving Christ. At age seventy she had said the sinner's prayer with Brian. Of course he misses her, but Brian says that grief is lightened because he knows his mother died "with her heart secure in Jesus Christ."

In his community service work, Brian has accumulated a number of photographic mementos of the many people his ministries has helped. He says he treasures them, but stresses that none of those images "is as dear to me as the picture of all thirty-four family members who, after much prayer and a little witnessing, were impacted by a great God who has this deep desire 'that none should perish, but have eternal life'!" (John 3:16).

Saving Grace for a Dying Uncle, and the Filipino Businessman

I'll close with a couple true stories of God's salvation knowing no limits. He can touch hearts anytime, anywhere—in a hospital bed or at thirty thousand feet, inside the cabin of a jet airliner.

A few years ago, I was visiting my mother in Wisconsin. It was a beautiful Saturday morning when I drove the forty minutes from Green Bay to her home, looking forward to playing a few hands of cribbage with her. As we prayed and talked, I learned her favorite brother, my Uncle Kelvin, was dying from lung cancer, caused by his years of exposure to asbestos. He was in his final days in hospice care at home.

Our family is huge. Mom came from a brood of sixteen, with untold numbers of grandchildren, great-grandchildren, cousins, and other relatives. I suspect our extended family could cause a shutdown on one of those Internet genealogy sites if we all logged on at once. But Uncle Kelvin was special to her and to me. He had been on my personal salvation prayer list for some twenty years, so I went to see him.

He was a nice guy, one of the greatest, most caring individuals you could ever hope to meet. He was religious to a degree, but not born again. I knew this could be the last chance for that to happen. When we arrived, we were warmly greeted by his family. I went over to his bed and took his hand; he was so weak he could barely squeeze it.

"Uncle Kelvin, I've been praying for you a long time. I know you go to church, but just going to church doesn't save you. I want you to be sure you're saved," I told him.

He rasped out his words in reply. He had watched me preach on local television in Green Bay, Wisconsin, and had even prayed the sinner's prayer I regularly offered at the end of each service. "I did that, but I'm just not sure."

So, we all prayed a simple sinner's prayer together, right there at his hospital bed. In fact, his whole family prayed it with him and even dedicated his baby granddaughter to the Lord. When we left that day, all of them finally had the assurance of personal salvation. We visited a bit longer, and then I left. Mom and I rejoiced all the way home about what God had done.

The next morning was a Sunday, and while I was greeting people before the service began I saw my mother walk in. Right away I noticed her eyes were red from crying. My Uncle Kelvin had passed away early that morning, she told me with fresh tears.

It was a bittersweet moment. We missed him, but we also were thrilled because he is safe in the arms of Jesus!

Be encouraged! God answers prayer—not always on our timetable, but He always keeps His promises.

The Lord seems to have given me special opportunities to share the gospel with people on airplanes. Here are a couple examples.

The first one involves a Filipino businessman. This fellow ended up seated next to a preacher as his jet took off from Chicago one hot Saturday afternoon in August. Yes, I was that preacher.

I was to speak the next day, so I pulled out my notes and Bible to prepare. My companion noticed this and asked what I did for a living. "I'm a pastor," I said, and as we talked and he learned what evangelical denomination I was in, his eyes welled up. He told me that was the same fellowship his sister had belonged to before she had died from Hodgkin's disease two years before. It was the same cancer that had taken my sister Judy's life.

Our conversation deepened, and as we talked it was apparent that this man had not asked Christ to be his Savior. As I gently explored that, he pulled out a letter his sister had written him before she had died—a final message that urged him to become born again; it even included a suggested sinner's prayer of repentance.

"Have you prayed this prayer?" I asked. He said he didn't understand it, so I had the opportunity right then to explain about Jesus' life, death, resurrection, and forgiveness of our sins. Soon after that, we prayed that prayer from his dead sister's letter together.

High above the midwestern plains that day, he became a believer. Someday that man will be welcomed by his beloved sister in heaven, her prayers for him having been answered from beyond her grave. I'll bet Judy will be there too, having made friends with his sister! I think she would have really liked this woman.

Finally, let me share my encounter with a fellow I will call Ken. I met him after spending a tiring, busy week preaching in Texas. When I arrived in Salt Lake City, I really just wanted to go home, see my family, and rest. But I had made a commitment to preach in Olympia, Washington, so I switched planes to continue on. As I folded my six-foot-four-inch frame into an aisle seat, I met Ken, who was sitting across from me.

Ken was on his way home to a small town outside Seattle. He was forty-six years old and had lived his entire life there. He asked me what I did for a living and why I was flying to Washington state; I told him I was a pastor and would be preaching there.

Now, it was my turn.

"Ken, are you a church man?" I asked. His reply was matter-of-fact but not impolite. "Well, no. I guess you could say I'm an agnostic, but my wife attends a [mainline denominational] church."

His wife's church happened to be the same denomination I had been raised in. I mentioned that and then explained I had accepted Christ, left that church, and joined an evangelical Christian fellowship. It turned out that Ken himself had been raised in a church that taught the born-again salvation message, but he had drifted away.

His mother had died, and his father still lived. Ken admitted his dad was always asking him to come back to the church.

"I guess when this life is all over, we'll both find out who's right," I said, referring to my faith in Christ and his agnosticism. Ken smiled, and we concluded our conversation—until we landed in Seattle and were waiting to disembark.

I turned back to him one final time. "Hey, Ken, it is Father's Day tomorrow and a Sunday. Why don't you go to church with your family?" I said.

He looked back at me and there were tears welling up in his eyes. "No, I think I'll call my dad and go to church with him!" Ken answered.

I am believing that is just what he did. I trust that it was God's plan for Ken, his mom, and dad to someday be reunited in heaven.

I believe that because God is faithful. He has made a promise that He will bring every one of those loved ones to the point of salvation if you do it His way.

Never, ever give up!

Notes

1. Bill Wiese, *23 Minutes in Hell* (Lake Mary, FL: Charisma House, 2006).

2. Ibid.

TO CONTACT
THE AUTHOR

arni@arnijacobson.com

www.ArniJacobson.com